APR. 03

Residential Substance Abuse Treatment for State Prisoners

Implementation Lessons Learned

Lana D. Harrison and Steven S. Martin

NCJ 195738

Sarah V. Hart
Director

Findings and conclusions of the research reported here are those of the authors and do not reflect the official position or policies of the U.S. Department of Justice.

The National Institute of Justice is a component of the Office of Justice Programs, which also includes the Bureau of Justice Assistance, the Bureau of Justice Statistics, the Office of Juvenile Justice and Delinquency Prevention, and the Office for Victims of Crime.

Preface

These evaluations of the Residential Substance Abuse Treatment (RSAT) program critique a Federal effort to encourage States to develop substance treatment programs for incarcerated offenders. The Corrections Program Office within the Office of Justice Programs provided invaluable support for both the RSAT program and these evaluations.

This publication offers program administrators the opportunity to modify or improve programs that are working well and adjust or discontinue programs that are not performing adequately. An evaluation may reveal that a program can achieve the goal it was designed to achieve with just a few modifications. It may also reveal that the program simply is not producing enough results to justify continued funding.

With the advent of performance-based budgeting and increased accountability to taxpayers, substance abuse professionals must clearly articulate and demonstrate—with data—how treatment programs for offenders can be successful and cost effective to the government.

Pilot programs can be set up so that their success or failure is measured through objective evaluation that will enable program administrators to learn which programs are producing the best results for the best price. Effective programs will prove themselves through data, and

program administrators will no longer have to convince the general population and government that treatment works.

It is important to collect program data carefully so that the data truly represent the program reality. Only accurate data can contribute to an effective evaluation. Program administrators must continually improve both their programs and their data collection and management procedures.

This publication will allow substance abuse professionals to share ideas. Those in one State can learn from another's successes or failures as they develop, implement, and evaluate programs. Increasing awareness of similar programs across the country will open new channels of communication. Objective program evaluation and open dialog within the treatment community—as well as publication of reports such as this—will enable RSAT participants to make new contacts, gather new ideas, and offer suggestions.

This report represents a significant accomplishment—both for the programs reviewed and for the RSAT program creators—and will be a practical tool in future evaluation efforts.

Richard Nimer
Director of Program Services
Florida Department of Corrections

About This Report

The prison population is at a record high, and most of these inmates have substance abuse problems. With this problem in mind, Congress created the Residential Substance Abuse Treatment (RSAT) for State Prisoners Formula Grant Program, which encourages States to develop substance abuse treatment programs for incarcerated offenders. Because of RSAT, intensive drug treatment programs have become the norm in correctional settings rather than the exception. Reductions in the costs of crime, criminal justice services, and health care services have shown that treatment is cost effective. This report summarizes the results of a National Evaluation of RSAT and process evaluations of 12 local sites across the country.

RSAT highlights

- RSAT has been responsible for substantial increases in the availability of treatment slots for offenders with substance abuse problems and in the number of staff trained to treat them.

- By the end of the 2-year evaluation, more than 13,000 inmates had been admitted to these programs.

- About 70 percent of the programs were aimed at adult offenders; the rest targeted juveniles.

Remaining obstacles

- RSAT programs experienced some start-up difficulties in locating and building facilities, recruiting trained staff, and contracting with treatment providers. Preexisting programs did better in this respect.

- Although research shows that aftercare leads to a reduction in reoffense rates, less than half of RSAT programs were able to include an aftercare component, largely because RSAT funds can be used only for residential treatment for offenders in custody.

- Many RSAT programs combined elements of one or more treatment types; such combinations, however, have not been evaluated and may lead to a "watering down" of treatment.

Who should read this report?

Corrections officials, substance abuse treatment providers, and Federal, State, and local policymakers.

Executive Summary

The Residential Substance Abuse Treatment (RSAT) for State Prisoners Formula Grant Program was created by the Violent Crime Control and Law Enforcement Act of 1994 in response to the increasing number of incarcerated individuals in the United States with substance abuse problems. RSAT encourages States to develop substance abuse treatment programs for incarcerated offenders by providing funds for their development and implementation.

RSAT grants may be used to establish or expand substance abuse treatment programs for inmates in residential facilities operated by State and local correctional agencies. To receive RSAT funding, programs must be 6 to 12 months in duration, provide residential facilities that are set apart from the general correctional population, be devoted to substance abuse treatment, teach inmates the social, behavioral, and vocational skills to resolve substance abuse problems, and require drug and alcohol testing. States are also required to give preference to programs that provide aftercare services.

All of the Nation's 56 States and Territories have RSAT programs. By March 2001, more than 2,000 programs were in place.

To test RSAT's effectiveness, the National Institute of Justice (NIJ) and the Corrections Program Office (CPO) developed an evaluation program that includes a National Evaluation of RSAT and 37 process evaluations of the local RSAT programs. The National Evaluation and the first 12 process (or implementation) evaluations completed are discussed in the following pages. The complete background and findings of these evaluations may be found online at http://www.ojp.usdoj.gov/nij/rsat. (Results of a third component of

the NIJ/CPO evaluation program—18 outcome evaluations of selected programs—are pending.)

Findings from the National Evaluation indicate that—

■ RSAT has been responsible for substantial increases in the number of residential and nonresidential treatment slots available for offenders with substance abuse problems and in the number of staff trained to work in substance abuse treatment programs.

■ By the end of the 2-year evaluation, more than 13,000 inmates had been admitted to RSAT programs, 3,600 had graduated, and 7,700 were still actively involved.

■ About 70 percent of operational programs were aimed at adult offenders; the remainder targeted juveniles.

■ About 70 percent of RSAT programs were for men, 12 percent were for women, and the rest were for both sexes.

Evaluators found that at the outset, many RSAT programs experienced difficulties in locating and building facilities, recruiting trained staff, and contracting with treatment providers. Preexisting programs fared better in this regard, perhaps because they had overcome their startup difficulties before the evaluation.

Unfortunately, administrative expediency and demands often took precedence over program operations. Programs were filled to capacity before sufficient staff were hired. Mistakes were made in referring inmates to the program and in matching treatment to their remaining sentences. The pressures of overcrowding often

meant that RSAT inmates could not be isolated from the general inmate population.

Despite research that shows that aftercare leads to a reduction in recidivism, evaluators found that less than half of the RSAT programs included an aftercare component, in large part because RSAT funding could not be used for aftercare programs.

The merging of different types of treatment was another concern. Most of the programs evaluated combined elements of one or more treatment types. Such combination treatments, however, have not been fully evaluated and may lead to a "watering down" of treatment.

Evaluators also noted the need for treatment options in jail settings. Jail-based offenders with substance abuse problems are a significant group, as the Arrestee Drug Use Monitoring (ADAM) program studies make clear, but the transient nature of jail-based populations is not conducive to a lengthy, structured treatment program. Jails should consider incorporating short-term education and intervention rather than long-term, phased treatment. Such programs require further investigation, but their absence represents a neglected opportunity to reduce drug use and recidivism among offenders.

Nevertheless, the evaluations showed that RSAT programs had made notable progress in overcoming their startup problems. Only a few programs seemed to be in serious trouble; established programs that used RSAT funds to expand their operations fared best. Thorough planning, a dedicated and experienced staff, and support from higher level administrators were all seen as crucial to a program's success.

At least until a pharmacological "silver bullet" is found, the only way to address the offender substance abuse problem is through lengthy and intensive behavioral intervention. RSAT promises to be a significant step in this direction.

Contents

RSAT for State Prisoners: A Major Federal Initiative

The Residential Substance Abuse Treatment (RSAT) for State Prisoners Formula Grant Program has had significant national implications for treating drug-involved offenders. Created by the Violent Crime Control and Law Enforcement Act of 1994, RSAT has encouraged States to develop substance abuse treatment programs for incarcerated offenders by providing funds for their development and implementation.

Although some noteworthy and well-publicized residential treatment programs for offenders emerged during the late 1980s and early 1990s (for example, Stay'n Out, CREST, Amity, and Kyle), the RSAT program represents the first national mandate or directive to affirm the value of treatment for criminal justice populations. With the prison population at a record high and substance abuse problems present among a majority of inmates, RSAT has the potential to help break the drug-crime link and significantly reduce the probability of relapse and recidivism for many offenders. Reductions in the costs of crime, criminal justice services, and health care services have shown that treatment is cost effective.

RSAT is helping intensive treatment programs become the norm in correctional settings rather than the exception. With the RSAT formula grant program in operation, every State has been offered an incentive to expand its residential treatment capacity and has applied for, and is using, RSAT funding to expand its treatment capacity. (See "Funding," page 2.)

All 56 States and Territories have RSAT programs. As of March 2001, more than 2,000 programs were in place around the Nation.

As a direct result of RSAT, therapeutic community treatment programs that had seemed unworkable or esoteric are now operating successfully nationwide, and corrections programs now regularly include a cognitive-behavioral component that encourages inmates to change their thinking and behavior.

Program characteristics

RSAT grants may be used to implement or expand treatment programs for inmates in residential facilities operated by State and local correctional agencies that provide individual and group treatment activities for inmates. RSAT programs also must—

- Be 6 to 12 months in duration.

- Provide residential treatment facilities set apart from the general correctional population.

- Be directed at inmates' substance abuse problems.

- Develop inmates' cognitive, behavioral, social, vocational, and other skills to resolve substance abuse and related problems.

- Require urinalysis or other drug and alcohol testing during and after release.

About the Authors

Lana D. Harrison is associate director of the University of Delaware's Center for Drug and Alcohol Studies, where Steven S. Martin is a senior scientist.

FUNDING

Funding for the RSAT initiative represented the largest sum ever devoted to the development of substance abuse treatment programs in State and local correctional facilities—$270 million over 5 years (1996 to 2000). The sums available for the program for each year from 1996 to 2000 were $27 million, $30 million, $63 million, $63 million, and $72 million, respectively.

Each State received a base amount of 0.4 percent of the total funds. The rest of the money was allocated on the basis of the ratio of each State's prison population to the total prison population of all participating States. States had to contribute 25 percent in matching funds. The grants are for 3 years and cannot be used to supplant non-Federal funds that would otherwise be available. The mean award to the States for RSAT implementation was about $450,000 in fiscal year (FY) 1996, rising to about $495,000 in FY 1997 and to $1 million in FY 1998; funding could be carried over to subsequent years.

The Corrections Program Office (CPO), Office of Justice Programs, within the U.S. Department of Justice, awards RSAT formula grant funds to the States and provides the National Institute of Justice (NIJ) with funds for evaluating the grant program. NIJ and CPO developed an evaluation program that reflects the range of RSAT programs.

States are required to give preference to programs that provide aftercare services coordinated between the correctional treatment program and other human service and rehabilitation programs.

Another important requirement of the RSAT initiative to States was to—

> ... ensure coordination between correctional representatives and alcohol and drug abuse agencies at the State and, if appropriate, local levels. This should include coordination between activities initiated under the Program and the Substance Abuse Prevention and Treatment Block Grant provided by the Department of Health and Human Services Substance Abuse and Mental Health Services Administration.

Partnerships were encouraged between evaluations, State departments of corrections, and RSAT providers.

Evaluation characteristics

The evaluation program developed by the National Institute of Justice (NIJ) and the Corrections Program Office (CPO) of the Office of Justice Programs has three components:

- The National Evaluation of RSAT.

- A set of implementation/process evaluations that examine individual RSAT sites.

- A set of outcome evaluations that extend some already funded process evaluations.

One goal of the evaluation was to assess a variety of programs, including those for adults and juveniles, males and females, and prisons and jails; programs based on different theoretical approaches; and programs conducted in different regions of the United States.

This report reviews findings from the National Evaluation, which documented the RSAT program through its midpoint, and the first 12 local site evaluations to be completed.

National Evaluation

Scope and funding

The National Evaluation was designed to track implementation of RSAT nationally using data provided by the States and programs. The evaluation was to include process and outcome elements that examined the types of RSAT programs and client characteristics, the impact of the RSAT program on treatment capacity and the costs of treatment, and the key elements of successful programs.

The evaluation team was also expected to identify promising programs for intensive impact evaluations, appraise the evaluation capacity of "State residential substance abuse programs," and enhance those capacities through feedback and technical assistance. NIJ hoped to develop a coordinated data set from the data gathered from the RSAT programs. Each State was required to cooperate with the national evaluators' requests for data gathering.

National Development and Research Institutes, Inc. (NDRI), under a cooperative agreement with NIJ and CPO, conducted the National Evaluation from 1997 to 1998. It used a series of three questionnaires to collect data from all the States and programs. Information was updated through March 30, 1999, for the final report.

The National Evaluation report provides a summary page for each State with correctional and treatment statistics for the State, a map identifying RSAT program locations, and a summary table of RSAT-implemented programs in the State.[1]

All 50 States, the 5 U.S. Territories, and the District of Columbia had developed plans and received funds for RSAT programs. By the time the evaluators concluded their work in March 1999, they had identified 97 programs that were operational or about to become operational. At midpoint, at least 70 programs in 47 States were fully operational and admitting clients. About one-third (35 percent) were located in medium-security prisons, 29 percent in minimum-security prisons, and 16 percent in maximum-security prisons.

Challenges

The evaluators experienced a number of challenges as they conducted the National Evaluation. Programs were continually coming online, and the numbers and types of programs and the characteristics of the clients they served were constantly in flux.

Because the RSAT initiative was rapidly expanding, new issues became apparent as the program matured. As a result, the evaluation's focus changed over time, and the evaluation ended without being fully abreast of all the activities in all the programs in all the States and Territories.

Treatment modalities

The National Evaluation identified three primary treatment modalities in RSAT programs: therapeutic communities, cognitive-behavioral approaches, and such 12-step programs as Alcoholics Anonymous (AA) and Narcotics Anonymous (NA).

About 60 percent of RSAT programs reported using some elements of the therapeutic-community approach. Some cognitive-behavioral approaches were reported by most programs, and 12-step programs also were nearly universal. Based on the responses to the evaluation's mail surveys, the National Evaluation categorized 58 percent of the programs as combined or mixed modalities, 24 percent as primarily therapeutic communities, 13 percent as cognitive-behavioral approaches, and 5 percent as primarily 12-step programs.

About one-fifth of the National Evaluation final report reviews treatment approaches in general. In practice, however, none of the approaches exists in pure form. Even the strictest therapeutic community incorporates cognitive-behavioral group work and includes 12-step meetings, and many therapeutic-community techniques (e.g., group encounters, reward and punishment, and phased programming) are used in other programs. (See "Treatment Modalities and Their Implications.")

Findings and lessons learned

The National Evaluation found that three-fourths of the RSAT programs were new; the remainder were existing programs whose capacity was expanded using RSAT funds. State officials unanimously reported that RSAT increased their State's treatment capacity for substance-abusing prison inmates. Although the States often provided information that was not comparable, the National Evaluation was able to conclude the following:

- Prison treatment slots increased from an average of 330 slots per year per State to an average of 400 slots over the 2-year evaluation period.

- Nonresidential treatment slots increased from an average of 842 in FY 1995 to 910 in FY 1998.

- The numbers of State treatment staff increased from 17 full-time equivalent (FTE) staff before implementation of RSAT to 26 by the end of 1998; the nonresidential staff mean rose from 16 to 22.

- A total of 9,600 treatment beds or slots were created.

- Although many programs had not yet opened, by the end of the evaluation period, more than 13,000 inmates had been admitted to RSAT programs, 3,600 inmates had graduated, and 7,700 inmates were still in RSAT programs.

- More than 860 FTE staff were providing treatment in 97 programs that were either open or about to begin by March 1999; the majority of RSAT programs were in State prisons, although 17 were in jails.

- About 70 percent of operational programs were aimed at adult offenders; the remainder targeted juveniles.

- About 70 percent of these programs were for men, 12 percent were for women, and 18 percent included both sexes.

TREATMENT MODALITIES AND THEIR IMPLICATIONS

Therapeutic Community

About 60 percent of RSAT programs were using at least some elements of the therapeutic-community approach at midpoint. A distinguishing feature of therapeutic communities is their use of the community as the primary method for facilitating an individual's social and psychological change. Another hallmark of correctional therapeutic communities is their isolation from the general correctional population. (The RSAT RFP required that therapeutic-community programs be set apart.)

The therapeutic community houses the inmates assigned to the program, a few professional staff members from the treatment and mental health fields, and recovered addicts, who serve a mentoring and staffing role. Residents are involved in all aspects of governing the therapeutic community and its operations. The therapeutic community is organized hierarchically with a clear chain of command. New residents are assigned to the lowest level of jobs in the hierarchy and earn better work positions and privileges as they move up the chain of command. They take responsibility for their own treatment and that of others. Groups and meetings provide positive persuasion to change attitudes and behavior, and group members are confronted by peers when values or rules are violated. Therapeutic communities try to socialize individuals, helping them develop a sense of personal identity and the values, attitudes, and conduct consistent with "right living." Most therapeutic communities today include additional services, such as family treatment and educational, vocational, medical, and mental health services.

Cognitive-Behavioral Treatment

Cognitive-behavioral treatment approaches are based on the social learning theory, which assumes that people are shaped by their environment. These approaches help offenders understand their motives, recognize the consequences of their actions, and develop new ways to control their behavior. Cognitive-behavioral programs are frequently augmented by training in problem solving, social skills development, and prosocial modeling with positive reinforcement. Although most evaluations of cognitive-behavioral therapy have been conducted with juveniles and young defenders, they consistently show substantial reductions in recidivism. Relapse-prevention techniques are generally part of cognitive-behavioral therapy and have been incorporated into all RSAT programs.

12-Step Programs

The 12-step approach, which views substance abuse as a spiritual and medical disease, began with Alcoholics Anonymous, but the principles have been applied to other drug and behavioral problems as well. Each program consists of 12 steps—specific graduated practices, beliefs, and traditions that progress from dealing with denial to sustaining a healthy, responsible, abstinent lifestyle. Although few research studies have evaluated the effectiveness of 12-step approaches with offender populations, they probably represent the most widespread treatment within the correctional system. This is partly due to their low cost, as they are typically operated by volunteers outside the prison. The National Evaluation found 12-step programs evident in about one-third of RSAT programs, always in conjunction with other therapeutic approaches.

Program difficulties

The most severe problems reported by State officials involved locating or constructing appropriate facilities, recruiting trained treatment staff, and contracting with treatment providers under lengthy or complex bidding and proposal processes. More than half (53 percent) reported moderate or severe delays related to difficulties in locating facilities for the residential treatment program, and 37 percent reported delays resulting from the need to construct or physically alter existing structures. About one-fourth of States (28 percent) reported encountering difficulties as a result of State regulations, and one-fifth (21 percent) reported delays due to State bidding or competitive processes. Nearly two-thirds (62 percent) of the States reported difficulties in obtaining training for treatment staff.

Lack of aftercare. The National Evaluation's report expressed concern over the lack of aftercare, particularly because the RSAT Request for Proposal (RFP) for States emphasized that in-prison programs with aftercare services should be given preference. Aftercare was not funded, however, and RSAT funds could be used only for the residential treatment component. The National Evaluation found that work release (23 percent) or halfway houses (20 percent) were incorporated as aftercare programs in less than half of the RSAT programs. A few others had parole-supervised treatment as part of aftercare, but these numbers were not reported in the National Evaluation. The National Evaluation determined that 86 percent of RSAT in-prison treatment programs have either specified how graduates may continue treatment in the community or indicated their intention to do so. Continuity of care is an important element in treatment for offenders and is strongly linked to reductions in recidivism and drug use.

Merging of treatment components. The National Evaluation also expressed concern over the merging of treatment components. RSAT programs are "intended to develop the inmate's cognitive, behavioral, social, vocational, and other skills," which lends itself to a multifaceted approach. Yet the evaluators pointed out that therapeutic communities, and 12-step programs in particular, are based on different theories and practices. The 12-step programs are spiritually based, which is different from professional therapy. Nevertheless, 12-step programs have worked in conjunction with therapeutic communities for many years. The National Evaluation accurately pointed out that combination treatments have not been fully evaluated and that many combinations may result in watered-down components, leading to less effective treatment.

Other problems. The National Evaluation showed that 55 percent of the RSAT programs lacked one or more operational treatment components, and 53 percent of program directors still considered their programs to be in the "shakedown" phase rather than stabilized at the RSAT midpoint. Programs had difficulty recruiting staff trained in the therapeutic-community and/or cognitive-behavioral methods as suggested in the RSAT RFP. Many States encountered difficulties employing ex-offenders and recovering addicts as counselors in prison therapeutic communities; often, individuals with criminal records were not allowed to enter the institutions to work or visit. Evidence regarding therapeutic-community staff effectiveness, however, shows that staff should consist of a mixture of recovered therapeutic-community graduates and other counseling (social work, educational, or mental health) professionals.[2]

The National Evaluation also pointed out that treatment programs should be in place in jails, not just prisons. About one in five jails reported a drug treatment program supported by paid staff.

National Evaluation shortcomings

In hindsight, it is easy to note problems with the National Evaluation's strategy of relying solely on mail surveys to gather program data. The study would have benefited from using other data sources, such as State block grant and statistical analysis reports. It appears that diverse research and evaluation interests led to very long and complex questionnaires, which resulted in missing data or inconsistent responses across States. The evaluators were unable to use survey data to determine the costs of treatment or States' contributions.

National Evaluation achievements

Although the National Evaluation was able to produce only a partial and preliminary picture of the scope and early accomplishments of the large national RSAT program by the time it ended in March 1999 (and any assessment of impact would have been premature), important lessons were learned from it.

The National Evaluation achieved some noteworthy goals:

- It presented a breakdown of the number, focus, and increased treatment capacity provided nationwide by the RSAT program.

- It provided a useful description of treatment modalities.

- Its recommendations included some useful and important suggestions for future treatment and evaluation.

Local Evaluations

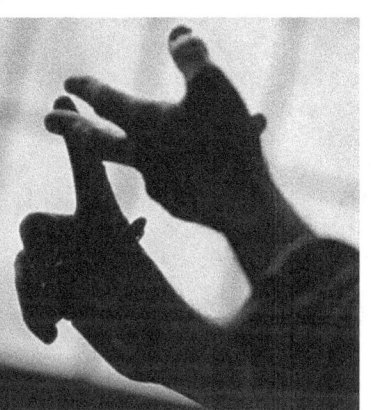

Scope and funding

In addition to the National Evaluation, 55 individual program evaluations were conducted. NIJ funded these State and local jurisdiction evaluations, which focused primarily on implementation of the RSAT programs. These program evaluations provide more specific and detailed program data. Brief summaries of the findings of the first 12 completed RSAT program evaluations are presented at the end of this report. It is beyond the scope of this report to establish how representative the 12 RSAT evaluations are of the 55 that were funded or to determine how well they represent the total array of all RSAT programs funded nationwide.

The 12 program evaluations summarized here were awarded between March 5, 1997, and September 30, 1998, causing the startup dates to be spread over 18 months. Some evaluators delayed their inception in an attempt to compensate for RSAT program delays. Others began their evaluations right away, even if their particular RSAT program was not operational. The awards for the local evaluations were scheduled to be for a maximum of 15 months each, while the RSAT programs themselves were funded for 3 years. Consequently, each evaluation represents a specific, varying, and only partial period in the lifecourse of each RSAT program that was studied. When one looks across evaluations, it is apparent that the time of study is often not coterminous from one evaluation to another.

Local evaluations either could look at a single program or, if a State funded more than one program with RSAT funds, could examine all or a subset of sites. The RFP requested information on program characteristics (such as number of participants, number of graduates, demographics, and other information about the participants) and "in-prison performance of participants on pertinent dimensions." The applicants were given discretion to propose additional topics. Each evaluation was expected to prepare for an eventual outcome evaluation. The fact that each evaluation covered different time periods and topics makes structured comparisons difficult, although a number of cross-site observations can be made. Many themes found in the National Evaluation were echoed in the local site evaluations.

Treatment modalities

All 12 of the RSAT programs whose evaluations have been completed established treatment programs that used a multi-modal treatment approach. Only one of these programs (the juvenile program in Michigan) did not indicate that it was a therapeutic community or that it incorporated major elements of therapeutic communities. Yet several that identified themselves as therapeutic communities or modified therapeutic communities contained too few elements typically found in such programs (e.g., the in-prison RSAT programs in New Mexico, South Carolina, and Wisconsin; the jail program in Harris

County, Texas; and the six Virginia jail programs); these may, however, evolve into mature programs. The programs in Delaware and Missouri are mature therapeutic communities, and the women's program in Washington State adapted a commendable therapeutic-community model responsive to women's issues. The RSAT programs in Wisconsin, New Mexico, and the six Virginia jails were not isolated from the remainder of the general incarcerated population, as the RSAT formula grant requires. All 12 programs included cognitive-behavioral elements and AA/NA meetings or 12-step philosophies.

Findings and lessons learned

The evaluations documented the many and varied demands and obstacles beyond the control of the RSAT programs. One of the most consistent findings across the national and local RSAT evaluations is the lack of effective aftercare programming. Several States had little or no aftercare, or aftercare was planned but not implemented. This was, in part, because the RSAT legislation explicitly precluded funding of aftercare programs. Yet recent research (much of it sponsored by NIJ) has demonstrated marked increases in long-term positive outcomes for offenders who receive both residential therapeutic-community treatment and an aftercare program.[3] The lasting effects from in-prison residential treatment alone, however, are not significant. Therefore, more attention to developing viable aftercare programs is necessary.

Few programs, even those that were fully staffed, delivered all the services they had planned (e.g., fewer group counseling sessions were held than planned and few individual counseling sessions were held in any RSAT treatment program).

Many programs experienced significant staff turnover, and programs were often initiated with inexperienced staff. Some contributing factors (such as isolated prison locations, poor pay, and the correctional environment's lack of appeal) are endemic to all prison employment. A slow process of gradually breaking in new staff and filling client slots, which is preferable for startup, often was not an option because of institutional overcrowding and the need to keep beds filled. Several correctional institutions have policies that discourage or deny employment to individuals with criminal backgrounds or to those in recovery. Because therapeutic communities are often staffed with a mixture of recovering therapeutic-community graduates and degreed professionals, such policies further limited the programs' ability to locate and retain qualified staff.

In light of high turnover rates, it would be beneficial to give greater attention nationally to providing training for correctional treatment staff. In starting a correctional residential treatment program, a full complement of experienced, well-trained staff is especially important. The required planning would have to be supported and implemented by administrators developing and overseeing a program.

Researchers noted the need for RSAT programs to use more valid and reliable substance abuse screening and assessment instruments. Nearly all programs experienced difficulties with inappropriate referrals—generally, inmates with too little or too much time remaining on their sentences. Some programs successfully matched sentence to treatment. For example, South Carolina created a novel RSAT program that based the incarceration period of offenders sentenced to the RSAT program under the Youthful Offenders Act on treatment completion. Similarly, in Pennsylvania, technical parole

violators were sentenced for 12 months to correspond to the RSAT programs' total of 6 months of in-prison treatment and 6 months of aftercare. Tying sentence length to treatment completion also motivated inmates to complete the programs in a timely manner.

Startup programs that tried to respond to the multiple and conflicting demands placed on them experienced most of the identified problems. Virtually all the programs experienced moderate to severe startup problems. The exceptions were preexisting programs that were expanded with RSAT funds (the Delaware and Missouri programs and, to a lesser extent, the Virginia and Michigan juvenile programs); these also had startup problems, but the programs were in a more mature stage of development at the time of RSAT funding.

The local evaluations documented that administrative expediency and demands often took precedence over program operations. Reported problems included the following:

■ Programs were initially filled to capacity although they lacked sufficient staff.

■ Staff members were inexperienced.

■ Inappropriate inmates were referred to the programs.

■ Clients were not isolated because of overcrowding and the need to fill all beds.

■ Graduates were returned to the general prison population when treatment was completed.

■ Inmates' demand for treatment was too great or too little.

■ Programs for dually diagnosed inmates appeared to be the hardest to implement because they also deal with the most difficult clients: offenders who are both mentally ill and substance abusers.

Major program transitions, where necessary, should be well planned before implementation is attempted. A program needs to be strong enough to survive the unintended consequences of bureaucratic changes. Even a mature treatment program or therapeutic community can be threatened by external program changes, such as new funding levels, reassignment of key administrators, and the actions of judges. For example, State bidding processes may mean a new treatment contractor is selected for an established program (as happened at one site). This example illustrates the need for strong institutional leadership to oversee and assist in the transition of treatment providers. It is critical that correctional treatment programs have outstanding support from higher level administrators who are committed to the program's success.

RSAT program achievements

The local evaluations emphasized the difficulty of establishing and maintaining a treatment program within a correctional setting. Even with adequate resources and excellent administrative support from the correctional system, program implementation was a tortuous process, and program stability was not reached for at least 2 to 3 years. It is notable that so many RSAT programs were doing as well as they were during early program phases and unfortunate that the local site evaluations were unable to encompass the programs' entire history.

A principal finding from the local evaluations was that many and varied demands and obstacles were placed on the RSAT programs. Their ability to survive and adapt when faced with obstacles beyond their control is more than praiseworthy. Only a few of the RSAT programs appeared to be in serious trouble. The

programs that fared best were established programs that used RSAT funds to expand their operations.

Both established and new programs benefited greatly when they had higher level administrative support and cooperation, which was essential to weathering many of the implementation obstacles. Programs with experienced and well-trained staff also had fewer implementation difficulties.

South Carolina and the Pennsylvania RSAT program for parole violators achieved commendable advance planning and coordination in sentencing inmates to treatment program completion. They reduced sentences somewhat to the length of the treatment programs, matching treatment and sentence length while saving the States some correctional costs. By tying sentence length to treatment completion, these programs eliminated the problem of returning graduates to the general population.

Several States had good aftercare programs in place, including the more established programs in Delaware and Missouri. One of the two Pennsylvania RSAT programs for parole violators had established the foundation for a good aftercare program; inmates flowed into halfway houses and their treatment plans were overseen by the in-prison program director. Good planning for aftercare was also evident in Washington State, and promising plans were being developed in a few other States.

Another achievement noted in many States was the cooperation between the evaluators and those involved with the program. Evaluators were able to feed information back to program officials and higher level administrators, who were able to respond to problems. Many evaluations adapted or created instruments and/or data management systems that they shared with program staff.

RSAT Success: Past and Future

Established programs that used RSAT funds to expand operations and those that received higher level administrative support and cooperation were the most successful at maintaining stable programs. It remains to be seen whether the increased capacity will be retained after the RSAT block funding to the States ends. The support of higher level administrators was essential to overcoming many implementation obstacles. If the State administration and prison officials were committed to treatment, the prospect was good—even for programs that faced major problems in implementation—that the program would develop, stabilize, mature, and become a regular part of the correctional system. Also, programs with experienced and well-trained staff had fewer implementation difficulties. However, various factors—including low pay, geographic isolation, and the correctional environment—made it harder for programs to find and retain experienced staff.

Another important observation from the national and local RSAT evaluations is the need for treatment options in jail settings. Jail-based offenders with substance abuse problems are a significant group, as the Arrestee Drug Abuse Monitoring (ADAM) program studies have made clear. At the same time, however, the jail programs that have been evaluated by the National Institute on Drug Abuse (NIDA), the Center for Substance Abuse Treatment (CSAT), and NIJ provide some understanding of the limitations of jail-based treatment.

The transient nature of jail-based populations is not conducive to a lengthy, structured treatment program based on community continuity and phased progression. (Therapeutic-community-type programs generally last 6 to 12 months.) Moreover, jail-based offenders are less likely to want treatment, and are less likely to perceive that they have time for treatment, than prison-based substance abusers. Treatment modalities should fit correctional mandates; jails should incorporate short-term education and intervention rather than long-term, phased treatment. Even relatively short-term interventions (6 to 8 weeks) can teach inmates coping skills that are crucial to recovery. Such programs require further investigation, but the absence of in-jail treatment services represents a neglected opportunity to reduce drug use and recidivism among offenders.

Two other major theoretical and practical concerns emerged from the local evaluations. First is the need to match the client with the appropriate treatment. Several local evaluations questioned whether the right kind of clients were being recruited into the programs. A growing literature is showing the importance of matching clients with the right kind of treatment and the implications of appropriate assignment in successful treatment.[4] Therapeutic communities are generally less costly than other residential treatment options because they rely less on paid professional staff. Twelve-step approaches have also been favored in prisons, primarily because

they are "staffed" by volunteers and because clients can continue participating in such programs when they return to their communities. It is important to identify the treatment modalities most appropriate for each type of inmate and the mix of elements that contribute to inmates' success.

The second area that needs to be considered is whether treatment should be compulsory or voluntary.[5] Compulsory treatment might work better than voluntary treatment for offenders. Holding out the possibility of a reduced sentence or tying sentence length to successful program completion can serve as the "carrot" that encourages more offenders to volunteer for treatment (as is the case in the Federal system—see 18 USC § 3621(e)(2)). Conversely, the "stick" might be increases in the length of time in treatment, which is the most consistent program characteristic associated with long-term client success.

Evaluation

The local RSAT evaluations demonstrated that it is possible to conduct a very successful evaluation that can have implications for research and treatment agendas. To do so, the evaluation needs a functioning program, good internal data collection and management, good working relationships between program staff and outside evaluations, and resources for evaluation.

Process evaluations can be very useful tools. Outside researchers, as neutral observers, are in a key position to provide feedback on issues and problems to administrators positioned to help create necessary changes. Although they require several years of data to be informative, process evaluations are not necessarily costly, especially in light of what they can bring to a program. Some of the local evaluations reviewed here did a good job of

process evaluation; others conducted only implementation evaluations.

Future evaluations of RSAT programs will require sufficient sample sizes, appropriate comparison groups, and sufficient time to conduct a prospective analysis to see whether successes are maintained over a reasonable followup period after release from prison. Longitudinal evaluations are necessary to evaluate programs effectively. Longitudinal process evaluations should be conducted for a minimum of 3 years, and outcome evaluations should be conducted for 5 years.

Aftercare

Clients who receive aftercare fare significantly better than clients who do not.[6] Several recent outcome evaluations suggest that treatment programs for offenders need a strong aftercare component and that the aftercare should probably be tied to probation or parole stipulations. One of the most consistent findings across the RSAT evaluations, both national and local, was the lack of effective aftercare programming.

The Office of Justice Programs might consider introducing a new initiative to fund aftercare for existing and ongoing residential treatment programs that have been sponsored by RSAT. A good aftercare program is not a cost-free option, but it would be much less costly per client than a residential treatment slot. This would be a cost-effective approach that would build on the residential treatment programs funded by RSAT.

Collaboration

One lesson learned from the local site evaluations was the need to plan, cooperate, and coordinate among criminal justice and public health administrators and

agencies. Such a model of collaboration needs to be replicated at the Federal level among agencies interested in treatment for drug-involved offenders.

In the early 1990s, NIJ, NIDA, and CSAT participated in several meetings at which the Federal agencies and their grantees shared information, findings, and strategies. It would be beneficial if these agencies and others interested in treatment for criminal offenders renewed their efforts and moved another step closer to real collaboration. The RSAT initiative and the programs that resulted from it represent a potential laboratory for research in treatment efficacy.

Treatment benefits versus costs

The connections between drug abuse and criminal activity have long been recognized. But only recently have policymakers acknowledged the efficacy of treatment in criminal justice settings. The past decade has seen some reversal of policies and practices, and many criminal justice professionals (police, judges, probation/parole officers, correctional personnel, and others) now serve as major sources of referral to, and payment for, drug abuse treatment.[7] The criminal justice system has become the largest source of mandated, or coerced, drug treatment in the United States.[8]

One of the classic questions in drug abuse research is whether the benefits of treatment outweigh the economic cost. Although different treatment modalities have different costs, the answer appears to be that treatment is cost effective regardless of the modality considered. Perhaps the classic study in this arena was published by the California Department of Alcohol and Drug Programs in 1994.[9] Known as the CALDATA (California Drug and Alcohol Treatment Assessment)

study, this 2-year investigation included a rigorous probability sample protocol of the nearly 150,000 individuals who received alcohol and/or drug treatment in 1992 in California. All treatment modalities were incorporated, including methadone treatment.

The estimated cost of treating almost 150,000 recipients was $209 million. Weighed against the cost were the estimated benefits amassed during treatment and during the first year thereafter; this figure was estimated at about $1.5 billion. Hence, for every $1 spent on treatment, approximately $7 were saved. Generally these gains took the form of reduced criminality and reduced hospital episodes. Criminality, from pretreatment to post-treatment, was reduced by two-thirds and hospital episodes by one-third. Nearly a 40-percent reduction was also realized in the before-after model in the use of alcohol and other drugs.

Also of note was the CALDATA finding that treatment efficacy did not differ by gender, age, or ethnic group.[10] Recent economic research suggests that the quickest and most cost-effective way to reduce the cost of drug abuse to the Nation as a whole is to treat chronic hard drug users.[11]

Additional implications for practice, policy, and research

Due to strict sentencing policies, criminal justice systems nationwide have received a growing number of offenders with significant and lengthy drug-using careers. Any prospect of changing this scenario requires effective substance abuse treatment for incarcerated offenders. Until pharmacological researchers and brain chemists find their "silver bullet," however, the only proven means of counteracting an offender's longstanding substance

abuse problem is a lengthy and intensive behavioral intervention.

In the late 1980s, the U.S. Department of Justice, through the Bureau of Justice Assistance's support of Project Reform and Project Recovery, introduced and evaluated innovative and intensive treatment programs. In the early 1990s, NIDA and CSAT funded a variety of new treatment approaches in correctional settings and evaluation of the programs. Most important, they disseminated and promoted successful treatment programs. The publicized success of therapeutic-community programs in California, Delaware, New York, and Texas was instrumental in turning policymakers' attention to funding and evaluating new offender treatment programs through RSAT.

One observation from the local evaluations is that the most successful programs (in the limited timeframe of these evaluations) are those that expand existing and relatively stable programs. It would be an easy mistake to infer that these are the better programs. That may not be the case; rather, these programs experienced similar startup problems, but they occurred before RSAT funding. In the case of the Delaware programs, the startup difficulties were enormous, and the programs might

not have survived except for administrative commitment, well-managed oversight, and very well-funded implementation budgets.

Several local evaluations were particularly instructive about the strengths programs need to survive when changes occur in treatment providers and institutional policies and leadership—the kinds of midstream changes that many correctional treatment programs face. State requirements about bidding contracts affect not only food services and health care providers but also treatment providers. Moreover, treatment programs have to be strong enough and sufficiently documented to survive changes in key personnel. Old-fashioned therapeutic communities with charismatic leaders rather than institutional leadership cannot survive long in a bureaucratic State system.

Conversely, a supportive system can be a real strength to a treatment program, particularly in its startup phase. Even when programs face major problems in program implementation, if the State administration and prison officials have a commitment to treatment, the prospects are good that the program will develop, stabilize, mature, and become a regular part of the correctional system.

Notes

1. Lipton, D.S., F.S. Pearson, and H.K. Wexler, "National Evaluation of the Residential Substance Abuse Treatment for State Prisoners Program From Onset to Midpoint," final report for National Institute of Justice and Corrections Program Office, 1999. NCJRS, NCJ 182219. (This document may be obtained from NCJRS by calling 800–851–3420. Documents under 25 pages are $10 each; documents 25 pages and over are $15 each.)

2. Wexler, H.K., "Therapeutic Communities in American Prisons: Prison Treatment for Substance Abusers," in E. Cullen, L. Jones, and R. Woodward, eds., *Therapeutic Communities for Offenders,* Chichester, NY: John Wiley and Sons, 1997: 161–179.

3. Lipton, D.S., F.S. Pearson, and H.K. Wexler, "National Evaluation of the Residential Substance Abuse Treatment for State Prisoners Program From Onset to Midpoint" (see note 1); Wexler, H.K., G. De Leon, G. Thomas, D. Kressel, and J. Peters, "The Amity Prison TC Evaluation: Reincarceration Outcomes," *Criminal Justice and Behavior* 26 (2) (1999): 147–167; Knight, K., D.D. Simpson, and M.L. Hiller, "Three-Year Reincarceration Outcomes for In-Prison Therapeutic Community Treatment In Texas," *The Prison Journal* 79 (3) (1999): 337–351; Martin, S.S., C.A. Butzin, C.A. Saum, and J.A. Inciardi, "Three-Year Outcomes of Therapeutic Community Treatment for Drug-Involved Offenders in Delaware: From Prison to Work Release to Aftercare," *The Prison Journal* 79 (3) (1999): 294–320.

4. De Leon, G., G. Melnick, D. Kressel, and N. Jainchill, "Circumstances, Motivation, Readiness, and Suitability (the CMRS Scales): Predicting Retention in Therapeutic Community Treatment," *American Journal of Drug and Alcohol Abuse* 20 (4) (1994): 495–515.

5. Leukefeld, C.G., and F.M. Tims, "Compulsory Treatment: A Review of the Findings," in C.G. Leukefeld and F.M. Tims (eds.), *Compulsory Treatment of Drug Abuse: Research and Clinical Practice* (NIDA research monograph 86). Rockville, MD: U.S.

Department of Health and Human Services, 1988: 236–254; De Leon, G., J.A. Inciardi, and S.S. Martin, "Residential Drug Treatment Research: Are Conventional Control Designs Appropriate for Assessing Treatment Effectiveness?" *Journal of Psychoactive Drugs* 27 (1) (1995): 85–92.

6. Pearson, F.S., and D.S. Lipton, "A Meta-Analytic Review of the Effectiveness of Corrections-Based Treatments for Drug Abuse," *The Prison Journal* 79 (4) (1999): 384–410; Wexler, H.K., G. Melnick, L. Lowe, and J. Peters, "Three-Year Reincarceration Outcomes for Amity In-Prison Therapeutic Community and Aftercare in California," *The Prison Journal* 79 (3) (1999): 321–336; Knight, K., D.D. Simpson, and M.L. Hiller, "Three-Year Reincarceration Outcomes for In-Prison Therapeutic Community Treatment in Texas" (see note 3); Martin, S.S., C.A. Butzin, C.A. Saum, and J.A. Inciardi, "Three-Year Outcomes of Therapeutic Community Treatment for Drug-Involved Offenders in Delaware: From Prison to Work Release to Aftercare" (see note 3).

7. O'Brien, C.P., and A.T. McLellan, "Myths About the Treatment of Addiction," *The Lancet* 347 (8996) (1996): 237–240.

8. National Institute on Drug Abuse, *Extent and Adequacy of Insurance Coverage for Substance Abuse Services* (Institute of Medicine Report: Treating Drug Problems), Drug Abuse Services Research Series, No. 2, Vol. 1, Bethesda, MD: National Institute on Drug Abuse, 1992.

9. Gerstein, D.R., R.A. Johnson, H.J. Harwood, D. Fountain, N. Suter, and K. Malloy, *Evaluating Recovery Services: The California Drug and Alcohol Treatment Assessment (CALDATA),* Sacramento, CA: California Department of Alcohol and Drug Programs, 1994.

10. Ibid.

11. Caulkins, J.P., and Reuter, P. "Setting Goals for Drug Policy: Harm Reduction or Use Reduction?" *Addiction* 92 (9) (1997): 1143–1150.

Appendix: Summaries of Completed Local Evaluations

Copies of the reports summarized below are available for a fee from the National Criminal Justice Reference Service by calling 800–851–3420. Documents under 25 pages are $10 each; documents 25 pages and over are $15 each. The individual site reports also are posted online at http://www.ojp.usdoj.gov/nij/rsat.

Delaware

Factors Affecting Client Motivation in Therapeutic Community Treatment for Offenders in Delaware (NCJ 182358). An expansion of the residential components of an existing continuum of therapeutic-community treatment in prisons, work release, and parole settings. Journal articles summarize a series of outcome studies. Programs operated in seven facilities, and each program was isolated from the rest of the facility. Staffing was reasonably stable, programs were licensed, staff met State certification requirements, and the programs were highly functional.

Michigan

Process Evaluation of an RSAT Program for State Prisoners: The W.J. Maxey Boys Training School (NCJ 182358). An expansion of substance abuse treatment services at Michigan's most secure facility for adjudicated male delinquents. Despite the program's thorough advance planning and smooth implementation, fewer services than intended were delivered, and inmates were taking longer than expected to complete the program.

Process Evaluation of the Michigan Department of Corrections' RSAT Program (NCJ 181650). A treatment program for males in a minimum-security prison based on the cognitive-behavioral approach, which included a 6-month in-prison component followed by mandatory 12-month aftercare. Some parts of the program, such as individual counseling sessions and AA/NA meetings, were not implemented during the evaluation. Other difficulties included communication problems with the aftercare provider (who was subsequently terminated), staffing delays, and a shortage of bed space.

Missouri

Report of a Process Evaluation of the Ozark Correctional Center Drug Treatment Program: Final Report (NCJ 181648). Expansion of a well-established adult male in-prison therapeutic community started in 1993 with CSAT funds that has scored well on the national instrument for evaluating therapeutic communities. The report provides a process evaluation of three changes in the institution since the RSAT phase began: a change in the treatment provider, institution of a work-release component, and an abortive attempt to institute a no-smoking policy. These changes hurt the program in the short run, but it seemed to recover well.

New Mexico

Process Evaluation of the Genesis Program at the Southern New Mexico Correctional Facility (NCJ 179986). A modified therapeutic community for male inmates in the minimum-security wing of a medium-security prison. The program suffered from startup difficulties and was not completely staffed until the end of the evaluation period. Because of overcrowding, inmates not in treatment were housed with RSAT clients.

Pennsylvania

A Collaborative Evaluation of Pennsylvania's Program for Drug-Involved Parole Violators (NCJ 180165). Two in-prison modified therapeutic communities (one at a maximum-security prison and one at a medium-security prison) for technical parole violators returned to prison. The program consisted of 6 months in an in-prison program followed by 6 months in a halfway house with specialized treatment programming. Problems with program implementation and aftercare, especially in the maximum-security prison, were detriments to success.

South Carolina

Evaluation of South Carolina RSAT for State Prisoners (NCJ 181050). A modified therapeutic community in a medium-security prison targeting male offenders sentenced under the Youth Offender Act that incorporates elements of cognitive-behavioral therapy and 12-step programs. The program experienced many startup difficulties but also made great strides. Although more attention to aftercare was needed, the coordination of release dates with program graduation was exemplary.

Texas

An Evaluation of the "New Choices" Substance Abuse Program in the Harris County Jail, Houston, TX (NCJ 182364). A modified therapeutic community (with 12-step elements) in the Nation's fourth-largest jail. The program suffered from startup difficulties (changes to the physical structure and delays in hiring) but there has been progress in resolving them. No aftercare program is in place, but new discharge procedures have been developed and contractual agreements are being made for aftercare client placement.

Virginia

A Qualitative Examination of the Implementation Process at Barrett Juvenile Correctional Center (NCJ 178737). An expansion of an existing therapeutic community program in Virginia for male juveniles originally started with CSAT support. The program has gotten off to a good start and appears to have avoided many of the startup issues experienced elsewhere. Some concerns remain, however: Youths assigned to Barrett may not be correctly assessed or appropriate for the program, the program's family education component is ineffective, and the program contains no aftercare component.

Residential Substance Abuse Treatment (RSAT) in Jail: Comparison of Six Sites in Virginia (NCJ 182858). Virginia also used RSAT funds to establish six jail-based treatment programs in the eastern and central parts of the State. Although some of the programs claimed to be therapeutic communities, none could be characterized even as a modified therapeutic community. Program clients were housed with other inmates, staffing was low, and staffers were unable to deliver planned services. Most clients did not complete the program, many because of early release.

Washington

A Collaborative, Intermediate Evaluation of the Pine Lodge Pre-Release Therapeutic Community for Women Offenders in Washington State (NCJ 181406). A 72-bed modified therapeutic community for women (with special attention given to women's issues) in a minimum-security institution. The problems documented in the evaluation report are characteristic of a startup program. The plan seems to be a sound one (although the aftercare component has not yet been put in place), and the therapeutic model appeared to be well developed and evolving over time in response to needs.

Wisconsin

Process Evaluation of the Wisconsin RSAT Program: The Mental Illness– Chemical Abuse (MICA) Program at Oshkosh Correctional Institution 1997/1998 (NCJ 174986). A mixed-modality program in a medium-security prison. The evaluation found that the program had excellent administrative elements but had difficulty successfully treating dually diagnosed clients during a short 8-month program and in segregating RSAT clients from the general inmate population.

About the National Institute of Justice

NIJ is the research, development, and evaluation agency of the U.S. Department of Justice. The Institute provides objective, independent, nonpartisan, evidence-based knowledge and tools to enhance the administration of justice and public safety. NIJ's principal authorities are derived from the Omnibus Crime Control and Safe Streets Act of 1968, as amended (see 42 U.S.C. §§ 3721–3723).

The NIJ Director is appointed by the President and confirmed by the Senate. The Director establishes the Institute's objectives, guided by the priorities of the Office of Justice Programs, the U.S. Department of Justice, and the needs of the field. The Institute actively solicits the views of criminal justice and other professionals and researchers to inform its search for the knowledge and tools to guide policy and practice.

To find out more about the National Institute of Justice, please contact:

National Criminal Justice
  Reference Service
P.O. Box 6000
Rockville, MD 20849–6000
800–851–3420
e-mail: *askncjrs@ncjrs.org*

Strategic Goals

NIJ has seven strategic goals grouped into three categories:

Creating relevant knowledge and tools

1. Partner with State and local practitioners and policymakers to identify social science research and technology needs.
2. Create scientific, relevant, and reliable knowledge—with a particular emphasis on terrorism, violent crime, drugs and crime, cost-effectiveness, and community-based efforts—to enhance the administration of justice and public safety.
3. Develop affordable and effective tools and technologies to enhance the administration of justice and public safety.

Dissemination

4. Disseminate relevant knowledge and information to practitioners and policymakers in an understandable, timely, and concise manner.
5. Act as an honest broker to identify the information, tools, and technologies that respond to the needs of stakeholders.

Agency management

6. Practice fairness and openness in the research and development process.
7. Ensure professionalism, excellence, accountability, cost-effectiveness, and integrity in the management and conduct of NIJ activities and programs.

Program Areas

In addressing these strategic challenges, the Institute is involved in the following program areas: crime control and prevention, including policing; drugs and crime; justice systems and offender behavior, including corrections; violence and victimization; communications and information technologies; critical incident response; investigative and forensic sciences, including DNA; less-than-lethal technologies; officer protection; education and training technologies; testing and standards; technology assistance to law enforcement and corrections agencies; field testing of promising programs; and international crime control.

In addition to sponsoring research and development and technology assistance, NIJ evaluates programs, policies, and technologies. NIJ communicates its research and evaluation findings through conferences and print and electronic media.